FREMSLEY

Also by Ivor Cutler and Martin Honeysett

Life in a Scotch Sitting Room Vol. 2
Gruts

Other books by Ivor Cutler

Poetry:
Private Habits (*Arc*)
Large et Puffy (*Arc*)
Fresh Carpet (*Arc*)

Children's Books:
(*Illustrated by Alfreda Benge*)
Herbert the Chicken (*Walker*)
Herbert the Elephant (*Walker*)

(*Illustrated by Helen Oxenbury*)
Meal One (*Heinemann*)
The Animal House (*Methuen*)

Gramophone records by Ivor Cutler
Privilege (*Rough Trade*)
Jammy Smears (*Virgin*)
Velvet Donkey (*Virgin*)
Dandruff (*Virgin*)
Prince Ivor (*Rough Trade*)
Gruts (*Rough Trade*)

Other books by Martin Honeysett
'Private Eye' Cartoonists: No. 4 Martin Honeysett (*Deutsch/Private Eye*)
Honeysett at Home (*Dempsey and Squires*)
The Motor Show Book of Humour (*Gresham*)
Micro Phobia (*Century*)
Fit for Nothing (*Century*)
The Not Another Book of Old Photographs Book (*Methuen*)
Dr Fegg's Encyclopeadia of All World Knowledge (*Methuen*)
Animal Nonsense Rhymes (*Methuen*)
Witch Doctor? (*Century*)
Best of Honeysett (*David and Charles*)

Cuiusque stercus sibi bene olet

FREMSLEY *by* Ivor Cutler
with drawings by Martin Honeysett

A
Methuen
Paperback

Some of the tales in this volume
first published as *Cock-a-Doodle-Don't*
in Great Britain in 1966
by Dobson Books Ltd,
Branspeth Castle, Durham
This paperback edition first published in 1987
by Methuen London Ltd,
11 New Fetter Lane, London EC4P 4EE

These tales were first broadcast by the
BBC Home Services between 1959 and 1963

Made and printed in Great Britain
by R. J. Acford Ltd.,
Chichester, Sussex

British Library Cataloguing in Publication Data

Cutler, Ivor
    Fremsley.
    I. Title
    828'.91409   PN6175

    ISBN 0-413-15540-4

If you would like more information about
Ivor Cutler, his books and his records, please send a
large stamped addressed envelope (or three IRCs
outside Britain) to:
    Ivor Cutler Mailing List
    Arts Theatre
    Great Newport Street
    London WC2H 7JA

to the timid
— the truly and
constantly courageous

Contents

Preface

After a long and exhausting meeting
between the publisher, the illustrator
and the author, it was decided that
there would be no point in having a
preface. Indeed, it would be
pointless.

I.C.

The Saskia Copier

I was sitting copying Saskia in the Rembrandt room at the National Gallery, when a voice arrived from over my shoulder. 'What are you doing there, mister?' A beefy choleric man, his eyes snapping about with rage, covered in a triple-breasted strategy suit.

I turned, and my gaze met his tie. On it was a hand-painted scene of Pizza in 1832, and the stucco baroque was bursting for a coat of paint. Thoughtfully, I filled my hog's bristle with Prussian Brown, and in a few minutes the buildings were as good as new.

Clearly, the change was not altogether to his liking, for he carefully removed the thick woollen garment from his neck, rubbed it firmly against my beard, first on one side and then on the other. Whilst performing this task, he kept raising and lowering his alternate feet quite quickly.

Reaching casually for my hair cutting scissors, I removed the majority of my beard in one 180° snip, gathered it in my fingers and placed it, with but a moment's hesitation, on his broad brow.

Removing the top from his hip flask with a loud bang, he took a short swallow then poured the remainder on to my velveteen smock. Lifting his first rate lighter, he snapped it on, but in a trice a broad attendant was by his side. 'No smoking, sir,' he said firmly.

Raising my canvas, the man placed it equally firmly over the attendant's shoulders, right down to his knees.

'Poor fellow,' I thought to myself, 'Rembrandt upsets him.'

Taking his little finger in an eighth of a Nelson, I raced him round to the Rubens room, and sat him facing 'The Rape of the Sabine Women' to calm down.

The Shapely Balloon

'Mammy, I want a balloon.'

'A balloon? What do you want a balloon for, son?'

'To play with.'

'To play with? Do you think I'm going to lay out good money so that you can play with a balloon? Certainly not. Start again.'

'Mammy, I want a balloon.'

'A balloon? What for, son?'

'I'm hungry.'

'All right. Here's 3d. Go and buy one.'

'Thank you, my mammy. [*pause*] Can I have a balloon please – shopkeeper?'

'What for, son?'

'I'm hungry.'

'We don't stock that kind.'

'Look here. Just give me a balloon. Here's my 3d. I'm hungry for a balloon.'

'Oh! No! Noho! We only sell them to play with.'

'All right then. I'll do it your way. I want a balloon because I'm hungry, but I'm going to tell you I want a balloon to play with, but you're not to tell my mother that I want a balloon to play with because she knows that I'm buying a balloon because I'm hungry for one. Do you understand?'

'Perfectly.'

'Good. Give me a 3d. balloon to play with.'

'Are you sure that's what you want it for?'

'Now look. We've gone all through this before. Give me a 3d. balloon to play with for goodness' sake and let me get out of here.'

'All right. What colour do you want?

'Any colour!'

'What shape?'

'What shape have you?'

'That shape – and that shape – and that shape over there – and this shape –
and that shape.'

'Give me that shape.'

'There you are – 4d.'

'But I've only got 3d.'

'I'll cut a portion off.'

'Then it won't blow up.'

'You want a 3d. balloon, don't you?'

'But it's no good to me as it is.'

'Of course it is! Look at the shape.'

'Oh, all right then, I'll take it. Mammy! I've got it!'

'Let's see! There's a bit off.'

'Yes. It's a 4d. one and I've got 3d. worth.'

'The man's a fool. Take it back and tell him you want a whole one.'

'He's not going to like that.'

'Tell him your mother said so.'

'I've brought it back. My mother says I've to get a whole balloon for 3d.'

'Look son, you wanted that shape?'

'Yes, I like that shape the best.'

'Well, they're 4d.'

'But I've got to have a whole one.'

'All right. Here's a shrunken one – right shape – right price.'

'But it's only the size of my thumb.'

'So!'

'I'm hungry for a balloon. That's not going to assuage my hunger.'

'Assuage? Don't you use these dirty words in my shop. Get out! Go on! Get out of my shop! Assuage indeed. I don't know what the younger generation is coming to.'

'Mammy, look. A 3d. balloon. It's the right shape, but look at the size!'

'That's not going to assuage your hunger.'

'That's what I said to the man and he got furious and drove me out of the shop and told me not to use these words. What'll I do, Mammy?'

'Why don't you sit down and shut up! Can't you see I'm writing your Aunty Mildred a poem for her wooden anniversary.'

The Electorate

'Hello, Fred who are you going to vote for?'

'I don't know, Bill. Who is there to vote for?'

'Well, there's Jack – and there's Dick, Fred.'

'Mm, Jack and Dick. What are they going to do for us, Bill?'

'I'm glad you asked that question, Fred. I'll tell you what they're going to do for us. First they're going to lower the taxis.'

'That's good.'

'Then, they're going to see that everybody gets a good education. Nothing intellectual. Just a good education, so they can fit into society.'

'Mhm. What next?'

'Everybody's to be equal.'

'Everybody?'

'Yes. Everybody, Fred.'

'Yow! Everybody. How about defence, Bill?'

'We're going to be so strong that them fellahs'll be scared to monkey about with us, but we'll be friendly with *them*, of course. This way we'll be 100 per cent safe, and our kids'll be 100 per cent safe too.'

'This is good stuff, Bill.'

'Now Fred, who you going to vote for? The ballot's secret you know. [*menacingly*] Who you going to vote for?'

'I'm going to vote for Jack.'

'Why Jack?'

'My grandmother's called Jack. Who you voting for, Bill?'

'Joe.'

'Joe? Which Joe?'

'My cousin Joe.'

'But he's not up for election.'

'Who cares. Joe did me a good turn during the depression. Kept telling me jokes and passing the Benzedrine round. My vote goes to Joe.'

The Thinker

'Pilot, what country are we over now?'

'Sir, we are over Zoobiostan.'

'Zoobiostan. This is where I get off. Stop the aircraft!'

'Very well, sir. Allow me to apply the brakes. You may jump now. Here is an umbrella.'

'An umbrella?'

'Yes, sir. This is an area of low pressure.'

'Hey, tribesmen, observe this one who descends from the sky at the end of an umbrella. – Hello!'

'Good morning.'

'Whence are you come?'

'An aeroplane.'

'Why are you come?'

'I have read many books about Zoobiostan and they tell me one thing: here, men are men.'

'And the women?'

'The women are men too.'

'Then why are you come?'

'I am come to think.'

'You must first use words with our chief. Chief, here is a stranger.'

'Greetings, stranger. Whence are you come?'

'An aeroplane.'

'And why are you come?'

'I have read many books about Zoobiostan and they tell me one thing: here, men are men.'

'And the women?'

'The women are men too.'

'Then why are you come?'

'To think.'

'What?'

'Deep thoughts.'

'You are a mining engineer.'

'Geologist.'

'What thoughts?'

'Emerald and amythyst. Thickstone, fumicestone and bauxite.'

'Men, remove this stranger's head!'

'Remove my head?'

'Yes. A man who wishes to think such deep thoughts must be left with his head clear to think, untrammelled by the cares of the body.'

'I bow to your will. It is Kismet. Chop away.'

'Have you a last word?'

'Yes.'

The Deoludous Nippers

Who has not seen the great twenty-foot Buddha which overlooks the reproduction counter at the British Museum? I visited it recently and became so excited by its sombre calm that my scalp contracted and a shower of dandruff fell quietly on to my respectable black suiting, causing many an amused smile among the habitués. Carefully removing my ballpoint and sketchblock from the lining of my respectable brown tweed jacket, I made a hasty, though thorough, sketch of the great image, then hurried home hastily, as fast as I could.

Peeling off my Chinese yellow shantung silk jacket and rolling up the sleeves of my pullover, shirt and vest, I elevated my balsa cutter and raced hysterically around looking for something to carve on. Finally, inside the meatsafe, I ran to earth a great lump of matured Madeira cake. I tested it diligently. Perfect! Not too soft to crumble. Not too old to crack. For eight months I laboured, and then – Eureka! – I was finished. I placed it on the place of honour on the mantelpiece – in a brand new blue plastic plate.

What now? I purchased a great lump of matured cherry cake and carved a Buddha, but a cherry came out on his right hip and I destroyed it, not wishing to be offensive.

Then followed a Genoa cake, a Dundee cake and a bas-relief on a cream cracker. Finally a seedcake. Then, exhausted after my four years of labour, I took a bath, donned my favourite silver lamé Cossack pyjamas and lay prostrate on the Gentian violet sofa.

Suddenly the phone rang. I opened the door and there stood five little girls aged between two and four, dressed in suburban party-dresses and scrupulously cleaned to hide their dispositions. The eldest advanced one dazzling white sock. 'I do declare! What exquisite Buddha-dollies.' And diffidently grabbing a Buddha each, they clattered down the long corridor shouting back promises to return them.

Their bird-like stupidity was like a toothache. Wearily, I closed the door on them to retrieve my own personal silence.

The Attic Chest

Everyone had gone out, so I took the ladder, propped it against the loft and climbed up, shutting the door after me. I switched on the feeble bulb. It was enough for me. There, square in the corner, was the attic chest. I ran up and gloated on it. The dirty brown wood and the rusty fasteners. I lifted it slowly, listening for the creak, then shut it again and lifted it again so that I could hear the creak again. An attic chest without a creak is like a flushing mother with a white face.

I shut it again and lifted it again. 'Creak!' it went. Aw. The beauty of it.

Then I peeped in. Yes. It was still empty. I stepped in and pulled the lid on top of me. The hasp went snap. Alone at last. I looked around. There was very little to see. It was pitch dark. I felt around with my fingers. The wood was rough unplaned poplar. In one corner was a knothole.

I took a deep breath, making myself as thin as possible, and slithered down the hole. I came out the other end and found myself on the attic floor. This wasn't what I'd anticipated, so I let out my breath till I was full size again and lifted the hasp, but it was locked and I couldn't get in. It could only be undone from the inside, so I took a deep breath and went back up the knothole into the box. To my great surprise, I wasn't in the box. I found myself on the roof. I began to quake. How was I going to get out of this unholy mess?

I slid down the roof till I got to the fanlight, smashed the glass and dropped lightly to the loft floor.

'Anybody up there?' came my mother's voice. I stood still.

'Anybody up there?' quavered my mother. I said nothing. I was too frightened.

I went up to the little hole inside the box, but I couldn't find it. It had gone. Covered with dust, probably. And as I couldn't get into the trunk, I was snookered and I've had to stay in the loft ever since. My mother shouts up now and again, 'Is there someone up there?' with a tremor in her voice, but I just walk around taking deep breaths.

The Tum-Tum Reader

I was seated at my easel on the Heath painting a landscape, when two women happened along. They stopped close by and started confabulating earnestly. Eventually the pretty one pulled the front of her blouse out and exposed her youthy stomach. The other peered long and earnestly at it, then shook her head sadly. 'I can't make head or tail of it.' Then they caught sight of me and trailed over.

'Excuse me, can you read...' the pretty one searched for a word that would make me think she wasn't common, 'can you read tum-tums?'

'Can I read tum-tums?' I said. 'Madam. I am an expert.' You should have seen the look of awe.

'Perhaps you'd care to read my tum-tum?' she asked diffidently.

'Delighted,' I shouted and bade her stand before me. You see, as an artist, a women's stomach causes me less embarrassment than a layman.

Then I placed a pair of spectacles on my nose which I use to frighten children away and proceeded to examine her stomach. It was the usual sort of stomach, you know, so I told her all the things that I knew she wanted to know, girls in their twenties are so unsure of themselves: eh, she was generous and all her friends liked her, she would marry a man who would buy her a house with a television, a washing machine, a fridge, two motor cars and a dish-washer. He would have a lot of money and he would be tall, rugged and blonde.

'Are you sure?' she said.

'Of course, of course,' I said. 'It's all written down there.'

'Well, my boy friend's dark,' she said, 'and if he reads that I'm marrying a blonde he'll half-kill me.'

'I'll soon fix that,' I smiled, and taking a large brush and my palette, covered her stomach with viridian green.

To my surprise, she started to cry and her friend ran off for the keeper. The keeper ran up and took my arm. 'Come along with me, mister,' and turning to the women, 'I'll see he gets what he deserves.'

When we reached the nearest pub we had a good laugh over a glass of yellow tansy. 'Paint my stomach green too,' he begged. 'I'll tell the old woman that the bowling green roller broke down.'

The False God

'Crawl up! Crawl up! See the famous god! Here you! Get down on your hands and knees! This is a god, you know!'

'Oh, no. Not me mister. I don't get down on my hands and knees to anybody.'

'Well, you'll have to, or else you'll have to leave the tent.'

'I've paid my money, sir, and I'm staying.'

'Come on now. Down on your hands and knees.'

'Look, there's no need for you to shout at me like that. I'm the only person in your tent.'

'Oh, all right. If you want to stand, keep right to the back, against the tent wall.'

'I'll do that. Now where's your god?'

'Take it easy. Don't be in such a hurry. It's behind this curtain.'

'Well, show me it. Come on. I'm in a hurry.'

'That's not the right attitude. Now you just stand quiet for a moment and I'll pull the curtain aside – There!'

'It looks like a gold brick.'

'It is a gold brick.'

'And you call that a god?'

'It's a good enough god for me.'

'Well it's not good enough for me. What else does it do besides sit there?'

'Oh, it talks to you.'

'Go on. Get it to talk to me.'

'All right. Wait a minute. Now listen – did you hear it?'

'No. I heard nothing.'

'You probably weren't listening on the right frequency. What frequency do you listen on?'

'Any frequency from 32 to 12,000.'

'Ah! Now my god talks on 20 to 22,000.'

'That's a damn silly frequency to talk on. That means that nobody can hear it except bats.'

'That's right. Nobody hears it except bats.'

'Then what are you asking me to listen to it for?'

'Well, you might be a bat.'

'Do I look like a bat?'

'No, frankly you don't. You might be a bat in disguise though.'

'Well, I'm not a bat in disguise. I'm a gold brick in disguise. And I accuse you of being in possession of a false gold brick. Here, let me see it. Just as I thought. A big lump of cod painted over. No wonder I couldn't hear it.'

Hens' Legs

You will have heard that a large consignment of hens' legs has arrived from Y'hup to-day. This is the first consignment of hens' legs ever to arrive from Y'hup and I may say that I am partly responsible for it.

You will perhaps think, 'Why have they only sent the legs? Why not the hens?' There is a sound reason for this. The hens are, strictly speaking, not like hens as we know them. In fact, they are known as Colomban hens, and it is a peculiarity of the Colomban hen that when you lift it up, its legs drop off. This explains the origin of the old Y'hupan song, 'How many legs have a Colomban hen?'

No one has ever been able to ascertain how many legs the Colomban hen actually has. People are always asking me, 'But when you lift up a Colomban hen and its legs drop off why don't you count how many legs have dropped off?'

The answer is quite simple. It is that the Colomban hen runs about Y'hup through the grass which is 18 inches high and grows thickly, with the result that when you lift the Colomban hen and its legs drop off – and they drop instantaneously – they drop amongst the grass. And people then say, 'It's worth a little time and trouble to search for them surely.'

My reply is, 'There are so many legs amongst the grass that it is impossible to tell which belong to one hen and which belong to another.' Then they say, 'Surely the old legs will be withered.' Curiously enough they're not. They're just as fresh as when they fall off.

The green rain is responsible for this. It appears to be its vitamin P content acting on the hen's leg arteries, plus the climate. That is why we were able to ship these hundreds of thousands of legs from Y'hup to this country. We did refrigerate them, but it was scarcely necessary, due to their coating of green rain.

As to cooking the legs themselves, I suggest that you soak them for an hour or two in rainwater. They will swell enormously – and then just eat them as they are. Don't heat them: it destroys their intrinsically tenuous flavour. Good eating!

My Jeopardized Farm

Ruined! Ruin stared me in the eye! The farm was in jeopardy. Only that morning, the old rural lawyer had pinned the notice on top of the notice board at the entrance to the farm, which had hitherto carried the proud legend, 'Eggs for sale,' with a great fat thumbtack. It read: 'This farm is in jeopardy.'

It was no use going to the agricultural courts. They would tie me up with their heavy obscure words, many of them obsolescent. No, I had to go. But I should sell the cattle and the horses first. Damn them! I shook both my fists at the ragged sky, then fetched round the lorry, laden with wooden packing-cases. 'Hoop!' I called. 'Hoop! Hoop!' The cattle and the horses came romping and curvetting into the yard. Dissolately, I packed them. First the cows, with their calves if they were still in milk. Then the bulls, and finally seventeen Kirkintilloch stallions with their saddlebacked mares. As I turned away to fetch a lid, one of the Kirkintilloch stallions leaped out of his packing-case and curvetted round the yard. The smoky sun gleamed on his glistening flank.

'You beauty!' I shouted. 'You shall be free. All of you shall be free! Hoo! Hoop! Hoop!'

The beasts rose as one from their snug packing-cases and made for the hills, where I could see them leaping and curvetting with satisfaction. Then I strode down to the notice, ripped it from its thumb-tack and sold an egg at a fat profit to a passing peasant.

Hitler's Tardy Hiroshima

'Come along, please. Hitler wants you.'

I squeezed along the corridor, passing many aristocratic military men and knocked gently on the familiar old pink padded door. Hitler opened it himself, and shook my hand in his friendly clasp. He wasted no time. 'Friedrich!' he called softly to his great blonde personal torturer. Friedrich padded over with a white hot letter E, which he applied to my ear, my elbow and my heel. 'Why my heel?' I asked, genuinely puzzled. 'You're going to London,' laughed Hitler, pleased that I had seen his little joke. 'E is for electricity. Tell me, are you brave?' 'Indeed, Adolf.' 'And are you strong?' For answer, I twisted the branding iron round Friedrich's throat and strangled him. 'You're my man,' said Hitler. 'I want you to go to London along the bottom of the sea dragging a cable. When you reach Charing Cross, earth the cable and you'll electrocute every Londoner in Greater London. Then come back and I'll make a great fuss over you – in public.' 'Adolf, you've always done the right thing by me; the job's as good as done,' and made my exit into the corridor, passing many aristocratic military men.

The following day, I entered the sea at Hamburg, literally coated with grease to keep me warm, and started the long drag across the sea.

A week later, I was well away and had time to think. I began to think of the Londoners. Did they deserve this? Well, they were our enemies, but under the sea I felt detached from the struggle and began to see England as the

magnificent people she was. Look at how she provided asylum for refugees: the Irish in 1845, the Jews in 1896, Indians, West Indians, Australasians, Canadians. What a record of tolerance! Every citizen a first class citizen.

I grew ashamed of my mission, but fortunately just as I reached Charing Cross, the War ended and I jumped on to the Embankment and became a first class citizen.

Tentwater

'Have you got the tentwater?'

'Oh, gosh...I forgot.'

'Go home and get it.'

'Go home and get it! We've gone 600 miles. We're nearly there. We're two miles from there.'

'Go home and get it. Didn't I say that we had to take the tentwater with us.'

'Yes I know, but we've only two miles till we arrive. There'll be tentwater *there*.'

'I don't want other folk's tentwater. I want my own tentwater. Go and get the tentwater.'

'Daddy! Daddy, I'm not going to go back th — —'

'Go and get the tentwater, I said.'

'Daddy. Come with me.'

'I'll sit here till you come back.'

'But I don't want to go 600 miles back home to get the tentwater. That's 1,200 miles altogether. And there's tentwater two miles away.'

'Look, son. I've always used my own tentwater. And your grandfather's always used his own tentwater and *his* father before him. Do you think we're going to take a stranger's tentwater now? Do you set no store by tradition?'

'No Daddy, but 1,200 miles.'

'I know how you feel, son, 1,200 miles is a long way. But can you imagine, if we went the two miles, and into the town, and they said to me, "Have you brought your tentwater?" and I said, "No. I left it at home. Can I have some of yours?" What would they say about us? They would say, "He hasn't got his own tentwater – his father had it, and his father before him – the stock's running thin!" – No, son. You've got to go.'

'All right, Daddy. I'll go. You wait here for me, won't you? I'll be right back. – Daddy, I've got the tentwater.'

'Already? 1,200 miles? How did you get there so quickly?'

'I ran as fast as I could Daddy. I didn't want to let you down.'

A Strategy Suit with a Jelly Pocket

'I should like a strategy suit with a jelly pocket please.'

'Strategy suits we have, sir, without jelly pockets. Ordinary suits *with* jelly pockets. Strategy suits *with* jelly pockets we don't have.'

'Well, I must say you seem indifferent to the needs of the public.'

'Nobody's ever asked me for a strategy suit with a jelly pocket before. A man who wants a strategy suit is a different man from him who wants a jelly pocket. Why not try next door?'

'I'll do that, and thank you. It's not often a tradesman recommends a rival – good afternoon!'

'Good afternoon.'

'I'd like a strategy suit with a jelly pocket please.'

'How dare you, how dare you come into a place like this – an establishment like this, for a strategy suit with a jelly pocket. I've been a tailor for three generations. You want a strategy suit with a jelly pocket? Go next door!'

'I've just been next door.'

'No no! *He* doesn't have them. Go one down! Don't come bothering me again unless you want a proper suit. By Jupiter!'

'Good afternoon, I'd like a strategy suit with a j——'

'I know what you want. You want a strategy suit with a jelly pocket, don't you? Try next door.'

'I've just been ne——'

'Not up there. *Down* the road. Next door.'

'All right. Why don't you——'

'Get out of my shop, quick!'

'Yes?'

'I should like a strategy suit with a jelly pocket.'

'I'm sorry sir. I've never heard of jelly pockets. We only do the normal kind of suits. Would you like to see one?'

'No no! It *must* have a jelly pocket.'

'Well. Try next door.'

'But I've just come from——'

'No no no no. Try next door, one down the street.'

'Thank you very much.'

'There's no shop there!'

'Oh sorry. Bang bang! Hammer hammer! There you are.'

'Thank you. Good afternoon.'

'I know what you want. You want a strategy suit with a jelly pocket, don't you? They all come to me for strategy suits with jelly pockets!'

'How did you know?'

'None of the other fellows in the street stock them. Keep sending them down the road till they come to me.'

'And do you *have* strategy suits with jelly pockets?'

'Of *course* I have strategy suits with jelly pockets. I'm delighted to do business with you, sir. What size of jelly pocket do you want?'

'About so big.'

[*Big laugh.*] 'Ah hahahaha! You'll never get a London tailor to sell you a jelly pocket that size. Not in a strategy suit.'

'Look, mister, I've got a big family of kids! I need a big jelly pocket.'

'Ah, ha, ha. I'm sorry. You see, a strategy suit's not strong enough to take a jelly pocket that size; not where the jelly pocket's being fitted.'

'I see. Well, what's the maximum size?'

'Oh, about this size.'

'Well, if you could make me one.'

'I don't need to make you one. I have one here made to measure.'

'Can I try it on?'

'Of course of course. Try it on. There. Perfect fit, isn't it?'

'Yes, it is indeed. Just as though it's been made for me.'

'It *has* been made for you.'

'What do you mean. I've only just come in here.'

'I'm a master tailor. Don't question me or I'll throw you out of my shop and you won't find a suit like this in London at a price like this.'

'How much is it?'

'Nothing.'

'*Nothing?* I can't take a suit like this for nothing. It wouldn't be moral.'

'Aw all right then. Give me ten per cent of the jelly.'

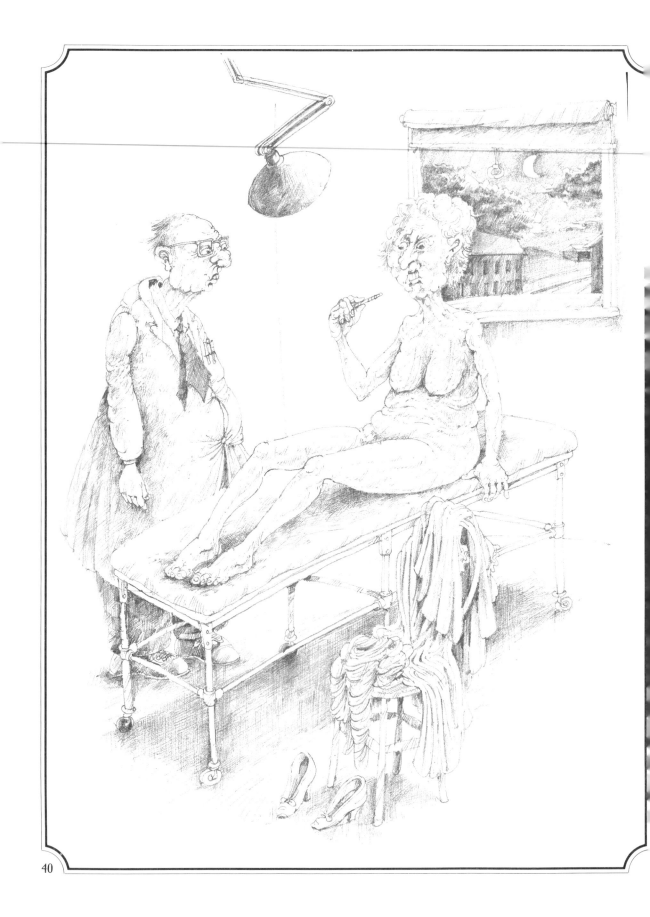

The Clever Night-Doctor

'Good evening.'

'Good morning you mean.'

'Good morning.'

'Good morning, what do you want?'

'Can I see the doctor?'

'He'll open the door presently, and then you'll be able to see him. In the meantime, what's your name?'

'Mrs Bigbuttons.'

'Just sit down Mrs Bigbuttons, the doctor will see you as soon as he has collected his thoughts.'

'Is he clever?'

'Clever – he's cleverer than a whole sackful of monkeys in a canvas bag.'

'Receptionist – send in the next patient.'

'Er, good morning missus, take your clothes off and get up on that trolley.'

'Do you mean that I ——'

'Look here missus, I'm a clever doctor. Didn't you see all my degrees on the brass plate?'

'No, it was too dark.'

'Receptionist!'

'Yes, doctor.'

'Why aren't my degrees lit up?'

'I was afraid to go out and light them up sir, it was too dark.'

'Well, come in earlier tomorrow before it gets dark and light them. Now, missus, aren't you undressed yet?'

'But doctor ——'

'Now look here, if you're not prepared to take my counsel, you had better find yourself another doctor – though I doubt if you'll find one whose surgery is open from 2.30-3.30 a.m.'

'I'm sorry, doctor.'

'There, that's better. Now lie down on the trolley and take my temperature. What does the thermometer say?'

'It says, "made in Venice".'

'Good. Now listen. [*sings unaccom.*] Go to sleep my Babby, close your pretty...receptionist!'

'Yes, Doctor MacBrazilnuts.'

'Wheel Mrs Bigbuttons away. Is there anyone else in the waiting room?'

'Mr Bigbuttons.'

'Tell him I'll see him tomorrow. Then lock the surgery door and come back and sing me to sleep. You'll find the music on top of my desk.'

This Man Want That Woman

'This man want that woman.'

'What for that man want this woman?'

'This man want that woman for marry.'

'This woman not want.'

'What for that woman not want this man?'

'This woman see no hair on head of that man.'

'That woman no like see no hair on head of this man?'

'This woman think that man got no hair on head, that man no strong.'

'This man come over to that woman. This man squeeze that woman. Ugh! This man strong.?'

'That man strong.'

'That woman marry this man?'

'This woman marry that man.'

'Oh, Mummy, Freddy's asked me to marry him.'

'How lovely, my precious. I'll iron your white organdie right away.'

Push-Kidney

'By gad! What's that across the road?'

  'Oh. That's a push-kidney. Haven't you see them advertised?'

  'No. I haven't seen them advertised. Oh. Look how big it is.'

  'Yes. I know. That's probably the de luxe model.'

  'Do they cost a lot of money?'

  'I'll say they cost a lot of money. Eh, I should imagine that model costs about twelve to fifteen hundred pounds.'

  'Twelve to fifteen hundred pounds for a push-kidney? Do you think it's worth it?'

  'Well – I don't know. I mean – there's been this demand created, I suppose, for push-kidneys, and people are buying them. And if you want a really good push-kidney then you have to pay twelve to fifteen hundred pounds.'

  'It's a lot of money for a push-kidney.'

  'I know. There *are* people who aren't buying them, but the pressure is enormous, and it's very hard to resist, when you see everybody else buying a kush – a push-kidney. People say "Have you a push-kidney?" and you say. "No, I haven't one yet. I'm just going to get one." And you feel such a fool.

You daren't say "I'm not going to buy one" or you'll be called an intellectual snob behind your back. When I see people with push-kidneys, I run round the corner till they've gone'.

'Yes. I get your point. I see just what you mean. Push-kidneys! Has this been going on long?'

'Oh, two years, three years.'

'As long as that?'

'Mhm!'

'And has the demand reached its peak yet?'

'Well, I should say it has reached its peak now and will continue along it for three months, then drop.'

'Mind you, it's jolly attractive, isn't it?'

'Yes. If you haven't seen one before. Naturally some people are a pushover for this kind of thing. For myself, I don't see any use in having a push-kidney. I mean my house is full of rubbish already, and, frankly, of what use *is* a push-kidney?'

'Well, of what use is a push-kidney? What's it for?'

'Ah-hahahahahahaha! He wants to know what a push-kidney's for. Ah-hahaha!'

The Fickle Sago Scrooper

Afflicted by insomnia, and having whiled away the hours reading a novel in which a heroine successfully engaged the attentions of a young man by lying at the foot of a hill with a crocked ankle in the rain, I decided to do likewise.

Living as I do in the centre of a hot plain, my detailed procedure differed.

First of all I prepared an enormous sago pudding, spread it evenly on the lawn on the north side of a shady larch, fastened my stays to the topmost branch, where they snapped and creaked in the convulsive wind, hammered at my ankle with a small billet of wood till it cracked, then lay on the sago and waited. An old man with a great smile on his face appeared. He pointed to the stays with his thumb and his smile broadened. 'Come to Glasgow, dearie,' he lisped. I gave him the outraged maiden treatment and sent him packing. Then a large pointed dog came sniffing along at my sago. I threw the billet of wood at him and he ran howling across the plain.

At last the man of my dreams sauntered along. His white brow was broad and his curls were the colour of chestnuts. 'Hello, big man,' I gulped. He lowered himself diffidently into the sago beside me and shot me a long look. 'What are we waiting for?' his eyes seemed to say, and he stretched out his hand and scrooped a handful of sago. For five weeks we lay there side by side, saying little, calmly scrooping sago pudding. Oh! The quiet bliss of those balmy nights! At length there was only one handful left. I handed it to him, but he pushed my hand violently away and rose to his feet. 'I'm off!' he gasped and waddled away into the rosy dusk. 'My ankle! My ankle!' I wheezed – but he was gone. I waddled sadly indoors and prepared an enormous semolina pudding.

Beatrice and Her Dirty Knees

'Beattie! Beattie!'

'Hello, Pop. You still awake?'

'I was waiting for you. Where have you been?'

'Out.'

'Out where? It's three o'clock.'

'I'm nineteen, Pop.'

'That's why I'm asking.'

'I've been out with a fellow.'

'This is all right, but three o'clock. You've been out late nearly every night.'

'I know. I'll try to come in early tomorrow. If you knew him, you'd understand.'

'Maybe I do. Who is it?'

'Fred.'

'Fred down the road?'

'Yes.'

'Fred with the blue jacket?'

'Yes.'

'But he's only six!'

'I love him, Pop.'

'Beattie, why don't you go with someone your own age?'

'You don't understand, Pop. The boys my age act like old men. They're tired, they don't know what they want or where they're going, they sit around as if the world's coming to an end. Fred: he's different. He's vital and sweet and raw. He knows what he wants. He wants *me!* He wants to be an engine-driver. He wants a dozen kids – six boys and six girls.'

'Daughter – Fred's all yours. He sounds a real nice fellow. Good luck!'

'Thanks Pop. Goodnight.'

'Goodnight – oh, Beattie!'
'Yes, Pop?'
'Wash the mud off your knees.'
'Yes, Pop.'

The Two Weary Professionals

'Bert!'

'Tom! Hello. It's years since I've seen you. How are you?'

'Fine. Fine, how are you?'

'Fine. What are you doing these days?'

'Teaching.'

'So you became a teacher, eh? I'm a doctor. G.P. I've had ten years of it and I'm weary. I'm weary, Tom.'

'Funny that. I've had ten years teaching and I'm weary too. Giving. That's what I've been doing, giving. I'm sucked dry. I want to get out of it now.'

'Me too. I feel I've done my bit for humanity and now I want to do something for myself.'

'Like what?'

'Like express myself.'

'Bert, you've said something that crystallizes what I've been feeling. I'm grateful to you. Let's go and express ourselves against this wall.'

'No, Tom, I've a better idea. Look down the road.'

'Ah, the post office.'

'Yes. Let's go and express ourselves to the south seas.'

'But how about Mabel and Betty and Clara and Ruth and Vera and the children?'

'Ah ha ha! Wake up, Thomas. Men aren't an economic necessity any more. And the children are old enough for it not to matter. Come on! – Two to the south seas. Express.'

'Here you are, sir. Stick this label on your forehead and go and stand in that corner. Not you. You're Tom the teacher. You're known as a good teacher. *Good* teachers are too scarce. I can't let you go.'

'But I'm *not* a good teacher.'

'Prove it.'

'I hate children.'

'Hahahahahaha! Who doesn't? Is that all?'

'I don't know the names of the five main glove-manufacturing towns in the Midlands! I've forgotten.'

'Then it's time you're out of the profession, Tom. Here, stick this on your forehead, and join your friend in the corner.'

'But it's daddy-long-legs.'

'I'm out of express labels. Tell the postman it's a pretend label. He'll understand.'

The Aimless Dawn-Runner

'Cockadoodledon't! Cockadoodledon't!'

I was running aimlessly down the country lane at 4.15, my ear cocked for the birds starting to sing when the cracked melancholy voice of the old man crouched on top of the six-foot English hedge arrested me. Slowing myself down, I arrived at a standstill opposite him. I held out my hand but he ignored it, choosing instead to flutter lightly down from the English hedge. Gently

saluting him on both cheeks in the Gallic fashion, I looked carefully into his face. It was the usual kind of face, except that the earholes were long and thick, odd in a man of his calibre, and a for-goodness-sake-cut-it-off moustache.

'Well?' I screamed, shaking him firmly out of sheer nervousness. 'Well?' The lettuce-green quality of the early morning light gave an unreal feel to the ridiculous situation.

'Cockadoodledon't! Cockadoodledon't!' he screamed back, and, raising himself on one foot, hopped over the hedge. I raced up and down the road till I found a gap and pushed through. I was in a farmyard. The old man was at the far corner. A ruddy farmer raced out through the farmhouse with a wooden cleaver through the chickens straight at the old man. *He* waited till the farmer was halfway then let him have it.

'Cockadoodledon't! Cockadoodledon't! Cockadoodledon't!'

The farmer stopped, poised on one foot with the cleaver above his head, like a fairy, then returned to the farmhouse, his eyes full of tears, absentmindedly gathering a few boiling fowls. The wooden door clicked shut. I turned to the old man. He was once again perched on the English hedge. I bent over to tighten my spiked racing shoes, then ran aimlessly into the lettuce-green dawn.

The Easily-agitated Pianist

'Excuse me, would you mind keeping quiet.'
    'Shut up, damn you, I can't hear the music.'
    'What's that you say? I didn't quite catch.'

'If you don't shut up, I shall call an attendant.'

'Do that then. Do that. Call an attendant.'

'I certainly shall. Attendant! Attendant!'

'So you called me then, madam?'

'Yes, will you please raise this piano.'

'I'll need to call two other attendants. I can't do it myself. I'm an old man, madam. You should feel my bones.'

'I can feel your bones. Just get off my lap, fetch two of your cronies and raise the pianoforte.'

'You said piano a moment ago.'

'I was agitated. I was upset. I'm sorry. Piano.'

'You mean pianoforte?'

'Yes. Pianoforte. Pianoforte. Now don't upset me any more or I'll get taut.'

'Madam.'

'Yes. Yes, what is it, you old fool?'

'How much do you want the piano raised?'

'A semitone.'

'Oh! I've raised pianos inches and feet in my time, and sometimes metres and vyorsts for foreigners, but never a semitone.'

'Well, now's your opportunity.'

'Madam.'

'Oh, my poor little nervous system, what is this trembling congenial idiot doing to you now. Whadda you want?'

'Don't be angry with me, madam. Please just tell me, why do you want to raise the piano a semitone?'

'I'm not really angry with you. I just can't stand you asking these damn silly questions. Anyway, I'll answer your question the Socratic way. Have you a

spirit level?'

'Yes.'

'Place it on the piano – what do you observe?'

'The bubble's dead in the centre?'

'What can you deduce from that?'

'Your piano's flat.'

'There. You've answered your question yourself. Now you can raise the piano with an easy mind.'

A National Disgrace

One morning at breakfast I made the mistake of complaining about the everlasting porridge. My father's thin lips tightened; the tips of his ears and the back of his neck turned as red as a peasant's leg, and his left nostril quivered. He reached over the table, yanked me out of my chair and threw me into the corner. After he had finished his breakfast, he took me into the barn and fastened me inside a large black cardboard sphere. Then he threw the sphere around. It never occurred to me to rail against this treatment. My father was, except on Saturday nights, an upstanding man and a pillow of the community.

One morning, I heard him roar 'Whar's ma black drawers?' to Mother, and I knew that he was donning his kilt. He came to the barn, saddled the cow, which we called 'Sauchiehall Street', because she never went faster than a trot, and we set off.

When we arrived, we were greeted with shouts of 'Kimera ha!' 'Chimera hay' and 'Ha pla!' It was the Highland Games!

When it was Father's turn, he raised me in my black box, and threw me. I landed in the river. There were great thick cries of 'Well, well!' I drifted downstream till I stuck on a sandbank in the middle of the estuary.

On misty evenings, as the fishing boats chug by, their holds tight with kippers, I call 'Ding Dong!' and the fishermen knock their heads sadly together and mutter, 'He complenned aboot the parritch.'

The Aggressive Onion-Vendor

'Put that down!' smiled the big woman.

'I was only looking at it to see where it came from,' I said.

I was in the market: in the fruit market and I'd lifted up an onion to see if I could see where it came from, but there wasn't any mark on it.

'Put that down,' smiled the big fat woman.

There was a queue of one or two dozen people behind me waiting their turn. The big woman was keeping her temper as best she could. Reluctantly I put the onion back on the pile. 'All right,' I said, 'give me half a pound of onions please.'

'A half a pound of onions,' she jeered, 'are you having a banquet or something?' I looked around at the other people. They seemed to be on my side.

'I don't like your tone missus,' I said. 'Do you want to serve me half a pound of onions or not?' She smiled at me. 'Get to hell out of here,' she said.

'I want a half a pound of onions,' I said, lifting up the onion again, and

looking around it to see if I could see where it came from. Her hand shot out, grabbed the onion out of my hand, put it back on the pile. Then she screamed 'Hey, one, two, three, four, five!' It must have been a secret call-sign, 'cause all the other people in the market left their stalls and came running up. 'Well, Betty, what's the trouble?' 'What's the trouble, Betty?' 'Hey, Big Betty, what's the trouble?' She pointed at me. 'He's making trouble.' Big burly man, with his sleeves rolled up to wrist-point looked at me: came striding over. Thick black hair matted his arms. 'Whadda ya want?' he rasped. I looked round. The queues had melted. There were only the stall-holders. It was getting dark too. I felt very afraid and alone. I burst into tears and ran away down the length of the market into the open street. Then I stopped. 'Am I a coward? Am I going to run away because a few burly people threaten me? No.' I walked slowly and firmly back up the market pretending not to see anybody, but I could see that all the people were back in their stalls again.

The queue was back. I went to the back of the onion-woman's queue to wait my turn. When it came my turn I looked her straight in the eye and said, 'A pound of onions.' She weighed me out a pound of onions. There was no trace of recognition on her face. I paid over my money, took the onions, and as I turned to leave the stall, she gave a great derisive cackle 'Ha ha ha ha ha ha ha!' I pretended that she was laughing at something else and hurried away, to gobble my onions furtively in a quiet lane.

Me and My Kid Brother

My brother and me are always quarrelling over the slightest thing, and you know we get so angry and we were quarrelling over a piece of bread the other morning, a little crust of bread that we'd found under the bed and there's the pair of us lying in bed, and one of us sees the crust under the bed. It was me or my brother I can't remember which and he says, 'Give it to me,' and I said, 'No. Let's half it. We'll have a half each.'

D'you know, we're to lazy to get up and it's not breakfast yet, so I said, 'We'll half it,' and he says, 'No, give it to me.'

'No. It was me saw it first and if you go on like this I'll have it all.'

And soon we were fighting and somehow he managed to get hold of the piece of bread: it was a crust from a piece of bread that either me or my brother a long time ago had eaten and the crust had gone under the bed. And he took this crust of bread and he popped it into his mouth and chewed it.

I got so mad: I was so furious that – that I hit him – punched him hard on the back. And this made him angry. He was half-choking. So I patted him on the back to relieve his choking and this hypocrisy – this hypocrisy engendered such a hatred in him that he jumped out of the bed, ran over to the wall and he started biting at the wall.

'Stop biting at the wall you fool.' But he didn't seem to hear me and went on biting, biting at the plaster.

'Mammy,' I shouted and I ran into her bedroom. 'Mammy,' I shouted, 'he's eating the wall.'

My mother sat up in bed. It's only half past seven yet. 'Aw!' she says. 'Leave me alone. Let me get back to sleep.'

'Mammy,' I said, 'he's eating the wall. He's eating the wall, Mammy. He'll be through the brickwork in no time at all.'

So she got up. She's weary. Weariness in every line of her nightie, her white nightie. And she came in with me to the bedroom, and we look at him.

There he is, my brother, biting away at the wall and he's reached brick now and he's still biting. He's furious and he knows that we're in the room because he bites more furiously than ever and he's reaching through the brick with his teeth.

'Stop, you fool!' said my mother. 'Stop it.' And she slapped him full on his ear.

He turned round with crumbs of brick on his lip. He looked my mother full in the face. His eyes were red with rage. He was so angry an excursion train wouldn't stop him. He went back to the wall, and he bit through – and do you know, he bit through the brick. Right through and you could see the daylight through the brick. Then he put his arm through and started to lever his arm about. Do you know, when he's angry he'll do the bravest things and won't mind hurting himself.

So my mother grabs hold of him. 'This is enough,' she thinks. 'There's a hole in the wall. What are the people going to see through the hole in the wall and she'll have to have a new brick in?' This makes her mad. So she stops my brother. 'Now! Enough! Enough!' And she took and threw him into the bed, which she could do quite easily, because my brother's only four, and I'm five. And she said, 'Now you stay there till I get up. I'm going back to bed for half an hour's sleep.'

And do you know, the pair of us got back into bed, and it was dead quiet and peaceful. We lay there like two mice. There was just the hole in the wall. We've never ever talked about it. I reckon he'd worked all his temper out. When I think back on it, it makes me want to cry, it was so calm and peaceful.

Mary's Drawer

Take your wellingtons off, children, and Mammy will tell you a pleasant story:

Once upon a time there was a pretty little girl called Mary. One day Mary's mother went to clean up the bedroom. She said to Mary, 'Mary, stay in the kitchen while I clean up the bedroom. Here is the kitchen drawer to play with,' and she bent down and handed her child the drawer.

'What shall I play at?' thought Mary. 'I know,' she thought, 'I shall play at boats.'

So she climbed on the sink, pushed in the plug and turned on the tap. Then she climbed down and sat in the kitchen drawer. The water soon came over the side of the sink, and in no time at all, Mary was afloat.

'I am a brave girl captain,' thought Mary as she sailed round and round the kitchen floor. But the water soon came in a tiny hole in the side of the drawer.

'Mammy!' shouted Mary.

'What!' shouted Mary's mammy.

'Come *in* a minute!' shouted Mary.

'Coming!' shouted Mary's mammy, then she stopped what she was doing and came into the kitchen.

'My boat's leaking,' said Mary.

Mary's mother took a piece of chew gum out of her pinafore and chewed on it.

'There!' she said finally, and slapped the gum on to the leak.

'Come and have a ride on my boat,' said Mary.

'Thank you,' said Mary's mother. She took off her shoes and waded through the water to the boat.

The time passed happily, then Daddy's key was heard turning about in the lock. He opened the door – and what a surprise he got when the kitchen

drawer sailed past with Mary and her mother in it, moved swiftly down the pavement and into the gutter, where it stopped when it arrived at the nearest drainhole.

'Ha! ha! ha!' [*spoken*] he laughed. 'You did give me a surprise.'

Mary's mother, whose name was Ellen, stood up and made her way through the crowd of laughing neighbours in stocking soles with the kitchen drawer and Mary to her kitchen door.

'You *are* a happy family!' bellowed Mrs Coutelier, a querulous old Frenchwoman who lived eight doors down.

That night, in bed, Ellen turned to her husband. 'Darling,' she said, 'I'm worried about Mary.' But Mary's father, whose name was Heinrich and who had to listen to this every night, pretended to be asleep.

The Magicless Half Leaf

'What are you doing there, mister?' I asked the great navvy, sprawled across the pavement outside South Africa House in Trafalgar Square. He shot me a beaming smile, and such was its warmth, I felt like a bus conductor having a bath. Lowering myself on to my flaccid paunch, my eyebrows twisted into question-marks.

'I'm watching this leaf, mate.'

'What's special about it?' I asked, squinting intelligently at what was surely a leaf of the common sapling.

'Turn your head,' he said. I did so. 'Now look,' he said. The leaf had changed its position. 'It moves of its own volition, mate,' he grunted.

I put out my hand to lift it, but was hampered by the fist of the navvy,

which had come down on my hand like a steam-hammer. 'It's mine, mate,' he smiled.

'I'll give you half a dollar for it,' I said. He stared unblinkingly at my left ear. 'Five bob!' No response. 'Ten bob,' I said, 'and that's my final offer.'

He stared at my left eye. 'Money can't buy this leaf!'

I went mad. I had to break this man. 'Ten pounds!' I shouted.

'Done!' he cried, and spitting into his hand, held it out.

'How quaint,' I thought and spat into mine and held it out.

'For half the leaf,' he added.

On these terms, we parted. I placed my half on the ground, turned my back for a second, then looked. It hadn't moved. Three times I tried, but in vain. Swindled! My ears went hot. I raced hotfoot after the navvy and caught up with him at Wapping Steps.

'Mine doesn't work,' I gasped.

He took the two halves and placed them patiently on the ground. I turned away, and when I looked again, only his half had moved.

'Hard luck, mate,' he said. 'All the magic is in my half.' I burst into tears. 'Don't take on,' he said gruffly. 'Come on, have a drink on me,' and grabbing me by the seat and the scruff, pitched me into the Thames.

The Perambulating Scottish Colander

It was a grey bitter day, the kind of day that makes a guilt-ridden Scottish family man say to his family 'Get your coats on. We're going for a walk.' Such was the wind, my body felt like a walking colander. To ease the situation, I left the main street and sidled furtively across the back streets. As I crossed a lane, my ear caught a croak. I looked up, and there, at the end of the long cul-

de-sac was a boy selling a paper. Some spark of humanity, that my environment had forgotten to quench, prompted me towards him.

He was wearing his sister's baby-blue crêpe de Chine nightie and a discarded grey cardigan of his grandfather. 'Let's see your paper son,' and I snatched it from his swollen fingers. It was an old copy of a paper that specialises in telling half-truths to half-baked intellectuals. I squinted at the lad. He was looking at me eagerly, as though my presence comforted him, so I read him the headlines. 'Floods in China, famine in India, America sitting in shelters, sexual abstinence the answer to over-population, says rabbit.' We burst out laughing simultaneously. 'Scotland's a grand country to live in,' he croaked, trying to hide his ungainly feet behind a stone. 'Why don't you try the main street to sell your paper?' I asked. 'I'm too proud,' he answered and took up that stance known and loved the world over, arms akimbo and lower jaw stuck out like a crumb tray. 'I'd buy your paper, but it's last year's,' I said. 'Good luck, however,' and I walked off, cheered by the encounter, heedless of the sharp stones striking the back of my head, propelled by the frustrated urchin, who was only human, like the rest of us. [*Laughter*]

The Spiral Staircase

'I want to buy a musical instrument.'
  'Yes. What kind?'
  'I don't know. It's for my son. He's tone daft.'
  'Why then do you wish to buy him an instrument?'
  'Uncle Wilfred has left him all his money in his will, provided he can play an instrument by the time he's twenty-one, otherwise the money goes to Cousin Mildred.'

'Perhaps the young man would like to choose one for himself.'

'Go ahead, William, see if you can find one you like.'

'I don't like any of them. It's you that wants Wilfie's money. You can't wait to get your dirty great talons on it.'

'Now that's enough, William, or I shall cuff you one.'

'All right. I want that one, then.'

'Which one , sir?'

'That one over there.'

'I'm afraid your choice is unfortunate. That is a spiral staircase.'

'That's the one I want. Mammy, I'm going to learn to play the spiral staircase.'

'Have you any music for it?'

'Here, madam.'

'This is a book of runs!'

'Yes, madam, this is the only music written for spiral staircases. Now, shall I send it, or will you take it with you?'

'We'll take it.'

'Shall I wrap it?'

'No thank you, we have the car outside.'

'Just a moment, Madam.' [*Shouts*] 'Hey you people on the first floor, don't come down. I've taken the staircase away!'

The Surly Buddy

James was a great surly workman – and my buddy. We had worked together in the pits, boy and man, for fifty-odd years. Done all the jobs: oiled the lamps, pushed the wheelbarrows, carried the coal. The pit we worked in had such narrow seams – anything between nine and eighteen inches, that the coal had to be carried by hand. The brubbies, special low trams for carrying coal along narrow seams, needed a minimum of two and a half feet. James and me had many a time worked our way back from a nine-inch coal face with a piece of coal firmly held in each hand, a distance of seven miles, to the main vertical shaft. This meant that it would take an entire shift of twelve hours to get to the coal face, pick a couple of bits of coal off the face and get back again. Our bodies and clothes used to get dirty working under the ground. As we stood in the pub on our way home with a quart in our hands we used to discuss our future. 'It's not economic to run the mine,' was the usual comment. All of us miners worked in the same pit, slithering about the narrow shafts, not a man of us under 65. No new blood. The last woman had left the valley fifty years ago, taking her children, but we clung doggedly on. You know, there's a challenge in a narrow seam, but not one of us would admit it, even in our cups. Reporters used to travel to the valley to try to get the miners to say something while they were in their cups, but as often as not, they got a broken jaw for their pains. We'd not been paid any wages for years, but gone around the valley selling the coal we won to one another. Coal was our currency. You wanted a quart, you slammed a lump of coal on the counter. There was no beer, only water. Mining's thirsty work, and a quart of water straight out a rainbutt is very welcome. 'James,' I said one day, 'I'm hungry.' 'Get yourself a piece of grass,' he replied, 'or a lump of chickweed. They're both outside in plenty.' 'No James, grass doesn't seem to satisfy me any more. I've a yearning for something tasty.' He turned his face up at me. The whites of his eyes were like yesterday's milk. 'I don't understand you, Ivor,' he said hopelessly, 'there's grass and there's chickweed, and there's rain in the barrel. What more

could the heart of man desire? Here we are, nobody bothering us, living a full life, and you say grass doesn't satisfy you any more. It's time you left the valley. You're old. You can't take it any more. Leave the valley!' 'I can't leave the valley. I'm an old man, James. You're the only friend I have.' But James took me by the shoulder and pushed me out of the pub and out of the moonlit valley, then turned his back on me and walked back to the pub. I daren't go into the valley. I just hang about the entrance hoping to catch James's eye. When I see him, and it's always night time, I lie down on the ground and slither about as if I was down the pit, to remind him how we were buddies. I'm getting hungry. I wouldn't mind a piece of grass, or even a lump of chickweed.

A Wag at the Flicks

'Please show me to a seat beside someone nice,' I begged the usherette and slipped her a florin. An old woman, and lacking moral integrity, she showed me to a seat beside an old man with his head back and mouth open snoring away. I stole a long look at him. Indeed. He was nice, but not quite what I had anticipated. When my eyes became accustomed to the dark, they roved around till they came to rest on a luscious morsel of feminity. Ah! I moved round and sat next her, my pulses racing with anticipation. I waited, my elbow on the rest, for 20 minutes, absolutely still. Then, sure enough, encouraged by my passivity, indifference and heavy breathing she brought her elbow in contact with mine. Oh bliss! I stretched my eager toe over to hers, releasing the trigger mechanism of the mousetrap fastened to my foot. She leapt 24 inches into the air with a noise like a Tory forfeiting his deposit in a rural constituency. The attendant scurried along. She saw me. 'You!' she sneered.

'He assaulted me!' squeaked the morsel, shaking like a loose tooth in a gale. 'I'm a woman!' I retorted indignantly. The attendant snapped on the lights. Everyone blinked and peered at me. 'I am,' I muttered feebly. The whole picture house roared, even the old snorer. 'All right. You're a woman. Just come and tell the manager,' said the attendant sarcastically.

I disengaged my toe, and strode shamefacedly into his office, shutting the door behind me. The manager let slip a book of what seemed to be holiday photos into the desk drawer, then rose to his feet in evening dress and well-brushed hair. He looked cheap and forbidding. 'Well?' he grated, breathing cafeteria at me. 'I'm a woman,' I said humbly. 'Prove it!' he rasped. I proved it, then left the cinema, my mousetrap snapping and unsnapping with each alternate footstep, to the great annoyance of the old attendant, lacking moral integrity.

A Big Head

'Mammy! Mammy! Look!'

'What is it? – Oh, son! – A big head! Oh, my son! A big head.'

'Yes Mammy,'

'All these years, son. And now ——— .'

'Yes, Mammy.'

'Come here, son. Come here and sit on my knee. There! Lean your head – oh, look at it! – lean your head against me – I'm so proud I could burst. Just a minute, get up a minute. Ahh! That's better. Now come back onto my lap and tell me all about it. Did you get it right away, or did it come in stages?'

'I got it right away. All of a sudden, I was popular!'

'Son! Popular!'

'Yes. You know I'd tried for years to be popular. Remember all the ointments.'

'Ointments?'

'For my pimples and blackheads. And the charcoal biscuits for my breath. And the sulphur skin soap and the dandruff cure that didn't work.'

'Ha ha, son. You were such a funny little hypochondriac. It used to give me a real thrill to see you searching through the women's magazines for free samples. The asthma cigarettes and the herbal tobacco. Phewff! You stunk the house out.'

'Well anyway, Ma, I came to realise that it wasn't my looks that were wrong, so I had a bash at my mind. Philosophy, psychology, sociology, pointillism. You know.'

'Yes, I know. I wish you'd get rid of these books. They give me the heebie-jeebies.'

'Ah, you never cared for the brain, Mammy. You didn't trust your brain. "Use your instincts, son," you'd say. "Your instincts 'll see you right." And you were right. I should've used them in the first place.'

'How son?'

'Well, that's what I did. My instincts said, "You want to be popular? Throw your money around." '

'You *didn't*.'

'I did. It was lovely. Everybody flocked around admiring me for this and that – and I got a big head – and my money's all done – and my instincts tell me that you've got some money stashed away, so hand it over or I'll bash your head in with the poker!'

'Oh, my darling son, you're just like your father.'

Fremsley

I was drawing pictures on the moist sweetie-shop window with my nose when
a sparrow tugged at my trousers. 'Come on!' he called. He held out a wing,
and I held it gently between my first four fingers. Then we ran down the street
till we came to the country. It must have looked incongruous, an old man in
cork shoes (I have fibrositis), running alongside a sparrow, but recently I
came across a book of photographs of old men in cork shoes running
alongside of sparrows. It was a Victoria book, so of course they must have
been young men, because of all the time that's past. The country was empty,
just grass about 100,000 miles except a hedge of hawthorn down the middle
with a ditch. We ran along the ditch Indian style, the sparrow in front. 'Stop!'
I cried. 'What's the matter?' he replied. 'What's your name?' I asked.
'Fremsley,' said the sparrow. 'Fremsley. That's a nice name – for a sparrow,'
said I, and we ran on till we came to a suitable bush. 'Here you are,' said
Fremsley, 'A suitable bush.' And we crawled under it and waited. Suddenly I
saw a commotion. 'I say, Fremsley, there's a commotion coming this way,' I
whispered. You should have seen him. He turned stone-white and shook as
though he had the ague. 'Hide me! Hide me!' he whimpered. I hid him under
my T-shirt next my heart. He dug his claws in and cocked his head feebly.
'Did you have a bath today?' 'Shut up! Here they are,' I whispered. A great
aristocrat burst into the bush with two slavering dogs. His gleaming black
taxidriver's leggings, his sagging khaki jodhpurs, his scarlet commissionaire's
coat with golden epaulettes like bathbrushes proclaimed him a man who could
extirpate a sparrow without mercy, or understate the interest earned on his
Post Office Savings Bank account to the Commissioners of Inland Revenue
without a gnawing at the vitals of his conscience. He pulled me out of the
bush, and, placing his pendulous mouth open by my ear, shouted 'Where's
Fremsley?' I shook my head. Who could compete with this well-nourished

man who was larger than Nature intended. 'What's that under yir shirt?' indicating the fluttering bird. 'Heart. Mitral stenosis' I muttered. He knew I lied. I knew he knew I lied. But I knew he would never reach into my shirt. He was a MAN. To save my face, he ran off with his slavering dogs bellowing 'Fremsley! Fremsley!' his dogs bellowing 'Fremsley! Fremsley Fremsley!' and they disappeared like dots onto the horizon. 'You saved my life,' sighed Fremsley. 'For better things,' I replied, and took him home and ate him for supper with chips.

Do You Believe in God?

'Do you believe in God, Tom?'

   'Yes, Bill, I do.'

   'Do you believe in God, Tim?'

   'No, Bill, I don't. I'm an atheist.'

   'Why, Tim? – No, no! Don't tell me. We'll have a meeting and let everybody hear both sides. I'll take the chair.

   Good morning, ladies and gentlemen, here are Tom and Tim to explain their religious beliefs. We'll start with Tom. Now, Tom, tell us, why do you believe in God?'

   'My parents believed in God.'

   'Thank you, Tom. Now, Tim, tell us, why do you not believe in God?'

   'My mother was an atheist.'

   'How about your father?'

   'Never mind my father.'

   'Come on, Tim, tell us.'

'Oh, all right. My father was busy earning a living.'

'But surely –'

'I told you, my father was busy earning a living.'

'Very well. Ladies and gentlemen, you have heard both sides of the question. The decision is now yours. If you believe in God, go out that door. If you don't, go out this door. Thanks, Tom and Tim – Wait, there's someone still sitting – Sir!'

'Yes?'

'Why don't you go out one of the doors?'

'I can't make up my mind.'

'Can't make up your mind? You're an Englishman, aren't you?'

'No.'

'Hey, it's my daddy. Hello, Daddy. What are you doing here? I thought you were busy earning a living.'

'I thought I was missing something. I came here to find out.'

'And didn't you find out?'

'No. I couldn't make up my mind.'

'Couldn't make up your mind? You're an English –'

'Don't *you* start.'

'Well, you'll have to go out *one* of the doors or else you'll have to stay here for ever, and we're going to lock the doors now.'

'Don't be daft. I'll climb out the window.'

'That won't solve your problem.'

A Wee Peep at the Ant-Heap

'Who's been eating the greenfly? The jar was full when I left the house.'

'Not me.'

'Not me.'

'Not me, Mammy.'

'Someone's been at them. Get on your feet all of you. Stand in a row. Now open your mouths – Huh! – You, Mollie, you! There's a bit of greenfly between your teeth. My own daughter! What did you do it for?'

'I was hungry.'

'You'd had your breakfast.'

'It's midnight, Mammy.'

'The impertinence! Take that! [*Slap*] and that! [*Slap*] Why didn't you say you had eaten the greenfly when you had eaten it?'

'I was afraid. You always hit me when I tell the truth.'

'Afraid? Afraid of your own mother? – So! A liar – and a coward too! My daughter. When I was a child, it was different. My mother and my father skelpt the living daylights out of me. But I always owned up. It didn't do *me* any harm, did it? – Well, did it?

The Youthy Rubbish-Judger

VIOLENCE AT LOCAL EXHIBITION

Although only four, I am something of an aesthete, thanks to my dad, but not my mum, who never once looked up at the sky when she hung up the washing. The other day, she unpacked a pair of execrable vases which would have graced any suburban lounge and bade me empty the shavings in the bin.

As the rays of the afternoon sun slanted into the bin they fell on the fresh-fallen shavings. What a thrill! The shavings pulled and strained at one another, just like a Cézanne – do you know what I mean? Let me put it this way – the shavings were juxtaposed in a resolved way that gave you the feeling you get when you feel a clock about to strike. Latent or suspended movement.

'I am going to take all the women in our street from their gas stoves and show them the wonder and beauty that lies at their own back doors,' I thought. Pulling a piece of French chalk from my trousers, I ran up and down the street writing in my sensitive scrawl, 'Empty your bin on the Green tomorrow at 9 a.m.' At 9 sharp, I dropped my hankie and the women, dressed for the most part in velveteen with fur revers, emptied their bins. What a stimulating sight in the cold yellow sun. Many bins were filled entirely with ash, which created, as far as one could see through the choking dust, a sombre truth. Mrs Ferguson, who bakes a lot, had a very pretty pile of eggshells. The majority had the usual mixture. The specialists were there of course – the butcher, the greengrocer and the hairdresser. But the bin which attracted me the most was a fine collection of gleaming empty spirit bottles. 'I award you the prize, Mrs McDonald,' I shouted, and handed the trembling winner a packet of peppermint drops. To my surprise, she caught me a slap on the cheek. 'You're a sad woman,' I said, and placed my arm round her shoulders. She hit me over the head with a bottle. 'When you're older,' said my mother as she dragged me home, 'you'll learn to let the Human Race alone.'

The Female Nincompoop

'Ah! There you are!' Jane entered the sitting room with a great posy of blossoms which she proceeded to shake in every corner of the room, as is the custom in our part of the country. 'Shake your blossoms in every corner, perhaps you'll find a handsome foreigner' runs the old saw. I watched fascinated as she tumbled my priceless Staffordshire figurines to the floor. The ritual complete, she swivelled her rose-red face on its alabaster neck in my direction. 'A dish of tea, master?' 'If you please, Jane,' and pointed to the marble wash hand basin. She filled it with China tea and placed it on my lap. 'What fools they are who dilute tea with water,' I thought, crunching a great mouthful of the coarse black aromatic leaves. Jane was still before me. 'What do you want, girl?' I sputtered through the tea leaves. 'Sir, tongues are wagging in the village.' Throwing the dish of tea to the carpet, I staggered to my brass telescope, through which I had been observing Jupiter's rings only the night before, and trained it on the village. Several tongues hove into view, all wagging. 'So! Will you marry me, Jane?' and clasped her hands round her throat, bringing a pretty purple blush to her cheeks. 'Ah, Sir, but do you love me?' she choked, writhing in her dilemma. 'Love you? A fine mature man of 87 love a nincompoop of 17? Of course I love you!' I shouted, sucking at a tealeaf that had lodged between my two teeth. 'Go and buy a trousseau!' and pitched a bag of gold at her. It caught her on the back of the neck. I applied my eye to the telescope. The tongues were still. 'There's nothing like doing the right thing!' I chuckled grimly to myself.

Back to the Earth

'Time we had a holiday.'

    'Yes, my dearest; where?'

    'I should like to go and do something different.'

    'All right. Let us go to that farm which everybody is raving about.'

* * *

'Excuse me, are you the farmer everybody is raving about?'

'Perhaps.'

'Perhaps what?'

'Perhaps I'm the farmer everybody is raving about.'

'Well, *are* you? Come on. We're decent ordinary folk.'

'If you're decent, ordinary folk, what are you doing on my farm?'

'We want the new kinky holiday. We heard.'

'It isn't kinky. It's a way of life.'

'That sounds kinky. We'll try it.'

'You've got to be there at least a week.'

'We're game.'

'Come then, into this field, take your clothes off, slip into these diaphanous plastic bags and lower yourselves into those individually-made holes. That'll be £40 a week, payable in advance, each.'

'That's pretty reasonable. Here's my cheque. Now go away and leave us to undress.'

'Not likely. I'm going to stay and watch.'

'It's O.K. dear. He's a farmer. He knows about nature.'

'I certainly do. Now – I say, your wife *has* a lovely figure.'

'I know. Everybody says the same.'

'Now, lower yourselves into the holes.'

'Which way do we face?'

'That's entirely up to you. I'll be back after a week and you can tell me if you've had enough. Just let me stamp the earth down round your necks. There. See you.'

* * *

'Darling, are you enjoying your holiday?'

'Yes, dear. Bit funny just your head showing and you naked underneath. Bet the worms and beetles'll be having a good look.'

'Let them. Anyway they're blind, so they can only see in the dark – It's a bit funny standing here in a hole naked in a plastic bag. Your face looks lovely in the setting sun.'

'So does yours. I feel this holiday's doing me good already – Darling!'
'What?'
'Are you tickling me?'
'No.'

Big Jim

'Help!' What an arresting voice. Such a rich timbre. Full and melodious. I wonder if it's a natural voice or whether its owner has had it trained. I'll let him call again. Perhaps I shall then better be able to tell. 'HELP!' Lovely! Rich and sonorous. But trained? I'll ask him to call again. 'Sir. Will you call again. I so enjoy the quality of your voice.' The man I addressed was floating precariously, just above the surface of the canal. Why! I recognise him. It's Big Jim. 'Hallo, Big Jim. How good to see you!' 'Ivor, you big twit, get me out of here. I'm drowning,' called Big Jim, with that poignant sadness in his voice that has all the fathers of heavily-built daughters from Troon to Aberfeldy shaking in their shoes. 'I'm wearing my good suit, Big Jim,' I replied, 'Please don't ask me to rescue you,' knowing as I was speaking that I should be forced to save this life, human though it was. 'Save me you fool, you'd have it on your conscience.' Even at this moment, Big Jim was in full

control of his facilities. He had me there, and knew it; knew he was safe on dry land already. I peeled off my clothes, even my string vest and pants, and plunged into the water. How soft it felt, like a housemaid's knee. It was 2′6″ at the edge, but towards the middle it was 3′6″, and 3′9″ in the dead centre where the barge keels had scraped a way for themselves when carrying a full load of pigsteel. I swam over to Big Jim and gripped him, and hauled him to the bank, and climbed out, and pulled him after me.

'You saved my life,' he grinned, and pushed me back into the canal. 'I can't bear to be beholden to anyone' Big Jim continued as my head broke the surface, 'So I'll take these,' and he strolled off with my clothes. One could hear the fathers of heavily-built daughters from Troon to Aberfeldy beginning to tremble again.

When it was dark, I left the soft water and ran stiffly home in my string vest and pants. They were already playing ping-pong in the orphanage as I passed.